ANTI-BULLYING
THROUGH
SPORTS

Anti-Bullying Through Sports

Anti-Bullying Through Sports

Copyright © 2022 Fredrick Spencer

F I R S T   E D I T I O N
Published in 2022

To order bulk or additional copies of this book, contact:

4J's SPORTS
www.4JsSports.com

Paperback ISBN: 979-8-9871710-0-4

Library of Congress Case Number
Spencer, Fredrick
Anti-Bullying Through Sports
1-11843630371 | October, 2022

Library of Congress in Publication Data

Category: Anti-Bullying, Athletic Coaching, Mindset, Motivational

Written by: Fredrick Spencer | 4JsSports@gmail.com | www.4JsSports.com | #4JsSports | #AntiBullyingThroughSports

Edited by: Dr. Linda Tucker | Cup and Quill Editing & Publication Services | linda@CupAndQuill.com

Transcribed and Interview by: Inspired Eagle Enterprise, LLC

Cover Concept by: Fredrick Spencer | www.4JsSports.com

Cover Design & Book Formatted by: Eli Blyden Sr. | www.EliTheBookGuy.com

Printed in the Tampa, FL, U.S.A. for Worldwide Distribution

Our Deepest Fear

Our deepest fear is not that we are inadequate.
Our deepest fear is that
we are powerful beyond measure.

It is our light,
not our darkness that most frightens us.
We ask ourselves, who am I to be brilliant,
gorgeous, talented, fabulous?

Actually, who are you not to be?

You are a child of God.

Your playing small does not serve the world.

There is nothing enlightened about shrinking
so that other people won't feel insecure around you.

We are all meant to shine, as children do.

We were born to make manifest
the glory of God that is within us.

It is not just in some of us; it is in everyone.

And as we let our own light shine,
we unconsciously give other people
permission to do the same.

As we are liberated from our own fear,
our presence automatically liberates others

– Marianne Williamson

Disclaimer

Limit of Liability/Disclaimer of Warranty: While the publisher and author have used their best efforts in preparing this book, they make no representations or warranties with respect to the accuracy or completeness of the contents of this book and specifically disclaim any implied warranties of merchantability or fitness for a particular purpose. No warranty may be created or extended by sales representatives or written sales materials. The advice and strategies contained herein may not be suitable for your situation. You should consult with a professional where appropriate. Neither the publisher nor the author shall be liable for damages arising herefrom.

*This book is dedicated to
victims of bullying, their families, coaches, and
athletes who have encountered and
witnessed bullying.*

May this book inspire hope for all.

Preface

Inspiration to the Victims and Families of Bullying

I see you, and you are loved!

I want you to know that I recognize the injustice you have endured and may still be enduring. I'm sorry for what you have experienced. If I could stand up for each of you and protect you from your abuse, I would. You have Survived.

Although some label you a victim, I encourage you to see yourself differently. Redefine who you are. Then allow that vision to drive your life going forward.

If you were victimized and are still here, you are not a victim but an overcomer. As an overcomer, you may remember what you have experienced. Rather than allowing the burden of those memories to weigh you down, imagine yourself as a victorious overcomer with a beautiful life ahead. Hurt and pain do not define you. Allow what you learned from them to help you create an extraordinary life. Don't let them go to waste.

Perhaps you are reading this book because a loved one, friend, or acquaintance was a victim of bullying and is no longer with us. This book is my way of giving back to victims. My mission is to educate people about the impact of bullying on the innocent. My goal is to help stop bullying altogether.

If you're fighting to stop bullying, I encourage you to continue your work. Your experience positions you to help others. I applaud your efforts to move forward with your life serving others. Take care of yourself as you take up this mantle.

As I work to promote change for the victims and overcomers of bullying. I'm also a survivor of and have witnessed bullying.
Therefore, I write for you from a position of empathy and experience.

– Fred Spencer

Table of Contents

BONUS

ANTI-BULLYING THROUGH SPORTS

by: FRED SPENCER

Introduction

Bullying is all around us; people are being pushed, pulled, shoved, criticized, mocked, taunted, and scorned. Some are scared to death, literally. They want to stand up for themselves or turn and run the other way. Unfortunately, many are so afraid of their attackers that they are paralyzed by fear. What does one do when fear holds them hostage?

Many youths face bullying. The term is relatively new. When people like former Presidents Bill Clinton and Barack Obama were younger and the targets of others, the term "bullying" was not in use. When children in elementary, middle, and high school were picked on, it was not seen as a big deal. People often ignored such harassment, leaving victims isolated and alone.

In this book, I discuss bullying and its impact on victims. My solution focuses on athletes and the actions they can take to help lessen the effects of bullying and, ideally, irradicate it. I encourage athletes, coaches, parents of athletes, family members of athletes, targets of bullying, and even bullies themselves, to read this book.

Bullying has detrimental effects on youth and teens. Bullied people often feel isolated and ashamed and may engage in acts of self-harm. My goal is to alleviate the problem so people do not experience such negative effects.

I am calling on athletes to use their platforms to impact the lives of others. I offer athletes an approach with offensive moves and defensive strategies to help recognize and diffuse bullying situations.

The book discusses why people bully others. Bullying has no boundaries. It does not discriminate against race, age, gender, sexual orientation, or socioeconomic status. Anyone can be a bully, and bullying can happen to anyone. You never know; you could be the one who brings a positive impact to another person's life. Keep an open mind as you read.

R·E·A·C·H

Ask of the Athlete: When you see this symbol throughout the book, let it remind you (past, current, and future athletes) there is something you can do about the situation. Trust me; after you read this book, you will see bullying everywhere. I challenge you to let this symbol show you how to help.

Hurt People – hurt people

                        - Dr. Sandra D. Wilson

Chapter One

What is Bullying?

Years of interacting with youth and their parents increased my awareness of situations among our youth. Traveling extensively as a former professional basketball player, parent, coach, and youth mentor, I consistently noticed many young people, some as young as nine, committing suicide because of bullying. I was teased from elementary to late middle school because of my poor reading and writing abilities. I was dyslexic but had not been diagnosed.

I work with youth in my community through various organizations in my chosen profession. While working around these future leaders, I hear about the difficulties and challenges they face in their peer groups. As I work to foster a healthy environment for youth, I realize this hurt is more widespread than one might imagine. It reminds me of the feelings of isolation, shame, feeling invisible, and self-degradation from being picked on about my reading and writing difficulties.

One day, I met a mother on a mission to bring light to the issue of bullying due to her personal loss. Her beautiful 13-year-old daughter, a middle school student, committed suicide because she was being bullied. As a mentor and father with kids her age, this loss of life hit home and became a personal mission. At that moment, I knew I had to do something: speak up and speak out.

To fight this fight, I had to educate myself on bullying. According to StopBullying.gov (a website of the US Government), bullying is "Unwanted, aggressive behavior among school-aged children that involves a real or perceived power imbalance. The behavior is repeated, or has the potential to be repeated, over time. Both kids who are bullied and who bully others may have serious, lasting problems."

After years of speaking to different groups, I am convinced that bullying has no boundaries, and victims are left feeling invisible and unheard. Bullying occurs across categories of race, age, gender, sexual orientation, and socioeconomic status; it can happen to anyone.

When I started this journey, there were four types of bullying. Now there are five. Often people witness but ignore bullying behaviors. Pay attention to signs of bullying and take them seriously.

Physical Bullying

- Hitting
- Kicking
- Shoving
- Spitting

- Beating up
- Stealing or damaging property

Verbal Bullying

- Name-calling
- Mocking
- Hurtful teasing
- Humiliating or threatening comments
- Racist or sexist comments

Social Bullying

- Excluding others from the group
- Gossiping or spreading rumors
- Setting others up to look foolish
- Damaging friendships

Cyberbullying

Misuse of information and technology intended to:

- Harass
- Threaten
- Embarrass
- Manipulate
- Exclude or damage another person's reputationor friendships

There is a difference between face-to-face bullying and cyberbullying. Face-to-face bullying often ends when school ends; there is no escape from cyberbullying because of social media and technology. It did not exist before the internet and social media platforms became prominent and readily available.

Sites such as endcyberbullying.org and blog.securly.com outline several examples of cyberbullying:

- Outing or Doxing refers to openly revealing sensitive or personal information about someone without their consent to embarrass or humiliate them. This behavior ranges from posting or sharing personal photos or documents to sharing an individual's saved personal messages in an online private group. The absence of a person's consent to share their photos or documents makes one a cyberbullying victim.

- Fraping is when a bully uses the victim's social networking accounts to post inappropriate content with their name. A typical example of fraping is a bully posting racial and homophobic slurs through someone else's profile to ruin their reputation. It can be harmless when friends write funny posts on one another's profiles. Depending on the content, such posts can be incredibly harmful.

- Dissing is when a bully spreads cruel information about the target through public posts or private messages. The bully tends to have a personal relationship with the victim, either as an acquaintance or friend. The intent is to either ruin the victim's reputation or relationships with other people by degrading and isolating them.

Sexting

- Sexting combines the words "sex"and "texting."
- It involves creating, posting, and sending sexually suggestive text messages, pictures, or videos of oneself or others.
- Sexting is usually done using cell phones, but people also use computers, webcams, digital cameras, and other electronic devices.

Bullying consists of ongoing, intentional verbal, physical, or cyber assault intended to humiliate and degrade a person (the victim). Not every unpleasant situation is bullying. Considering the causes and effects of certain behaviors is necessary to discern what is and is not bullying. We must not confuse bullying with behavioral issues such as disagreements, rudeness, or being mean. People may be mean or rude when the behavior and its effects are unplanned. In such instances, rudeness and meanness are not acts of bullying.

Stop Bullying on cyberbullying.org

Stop Bullying

Stopbullying.gov is an official website of the United States Government. The website offers a broad spectrum of information to equip advocates with information to help stop bullying. This resource suggests there are ways to stop bullying on the spot and prevent bullying by taking actions such as teaching children how to talk about bullying, creating a safe school environment, and launching a community-wide bullying prevention strategy.

"I allowed myself to be bullied because I was scared and didn't know how to defend myself. I was bullied until I prevented a new student from being bullied. By standing up for him, I learned to stand up for myself."

— Jackie Chan

Chapter Two

How to Identify a Bully?

This book resulted from my emotional journey, which involved educating myself about bullying. Among the questions I am most often asked are: "What does a bully look like?" and "How do you identify a bully?" This chapter addresses these questions.

Many movies accurately portray bullying. These include: Mean Girls, Carrie, Karate Kid, Cobra Kai, Bully, Moonlight, and Joe Bell. Collectively, the movies reveal that anyone can be a bully regardless of race, age, gender, sexual orientation, or socioeconomic status.

Resources such as StopBullying.gov offer insight into circumstances that cause people to become bullies and thus help us to understand common characteristics of bullies. Bullies bully for many reasons, including

- peer pressure
- a desire to feel in control and powerful
- an attempt to deal with low confidence and self-esteem issues
- the need to cope with anger and unhappiness
- having little to no empathy for others

Roles People Play in Bullying

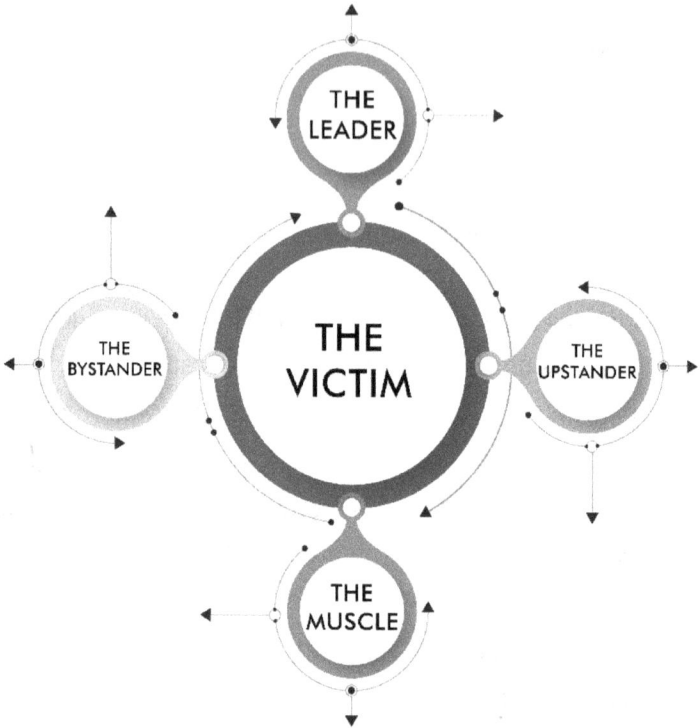

The arrows represent the phase: *What Goes Around Comes Around.* The role you are in today can change for you tomorrow.

Example: Bystander today | Victim tomorrow

The Leader

This person surrounds themselves with people who are followers. Followers are insecure, physically strong, and often view violence as positive. They select targets for the leader to bully. The leader may act as "the muscle," motivating others to begin or continue bullying behaviors. Leaders enjoy conflict and refuse to accept responsibility for negative behaviors.

The Muscle

This person will start the bullying after the leader chooses the victim. They may be the first to hurt the victim physically or verbally. Their attack encourages others to treat the victim similarly.

The Upstander

This individual recognizes the victimization and acts on behalf of the victim. The Upstander may slow down or completely stop the bullying.

The Bystander

This person may be at a bullying incident but not participate in the action. Despite their nonparticipation, they are involved by choosing to become spectators of the bullying.

The Victim

The person bullied is the unfortunate prey of the Leader and Muscle. The victim endures emotional, physical, or verbal abuse.

The Causes of Bullying

Bullies prey on their victims for many reasons. Unfortunately, anyone could become prey to a bully, but victims share common characteristics, including:

- Low self-esteem
- Learning disabilities
- Poverty
- Smaller frames, weight struggles
- Few defensive skills, so they don't stand up for themselves
- Newcomers to the area, school, neighborhood,or team
- Sexual orientation

Anyone can be a bully, and any situation can lead to bullying. No race or class of people is safe from bullying and its effects.

Effects of Bullying

Research points to the long-term psychological effects of bullying that may significantly impact victims' and bullies' physical and emotional health.

Over the last few decades, bullying has become a focus among researchers and recognized as a significant concern among school personnel, students, and parents over the past few decades. Research reveals substantial psychological repercussions of bullying. Those bullied have increased risks of depression, anxiety, suicidal ideation, and self-harming behaviors.

Earlier research frequently relied on data with little insight into bullying's impact on victims' mental health when they become adults. However, recent research reveals long-term effects. Alice G. Walton (2013), in "The Psychological Effects of Bullying Last Well into adulthood," discusses the long-term psychological impact of bullying on bullies and bullied children.

Researchers analyzed data from over 1,400 kids in North Carolina, ages nine to thirteen. The youth answered questions about their experiences of being bullied or bullying others. Some children fit into one category (bully or victim), and others identified themselves in both roles.

When the children were between nineteen and twenty-six, researchers reinterviewed them. Depressive disorders, anxiety disorders, generalized anxiety (e.g., PTSD, OCD), panic disorders, substance dependence, and antisocial personality disorder were more common among people who had been victims.

Those who were both bullying victims and bullies fared worse, suffering from various forms of depression and anxiety disorders, with suicidal thoughts and depressive episodes being the most common.

Adults who were one-time bullies (and never victims) did not have the same risk for mental health issues as those who were victims or victims and bullies. Instead, they had an increased risk for antisocial personality disorder. There were fewer connections between bullying and childhood psychiatric disorders, maltreatment, socioeconomic position, and family hardships.

Walton concludes, "Bullying is not just a harmless rite of passage or an inevitable part of growing up," despite the common misperception. The authors call for better intervention strategies and increased awareness of the serious effects of bullying, which will hopefully "reduce human suffering and long-term health costs and provide a safer environment for children to grow up in."

Focused actions are in order based on "how pro- foundly bullying affects a person's long-term function- ing," according to William E. Copeland. He adds, "This psychological damage doesn't just disappear because a person grew up and is no longer bullied. This is something that stays with them. If we can address this now, we can prevent many problems down the road."

Increasing awareness that bullying has no boundaries and happens all around us is essential if we're to end the suffering of those involved.

NAMI Helpline

The National Alliance on Mental Illnesson NAMI.org

The impact of bullying varies in intensity depending on its severity, duration, and individual responses to the experience. Preventing or stopping bullying among children gives them a better shot at becoming emotionally healthy and happy adults.

The National Alliance on Mental Illness (NAMI) Helpline is a free, nationwide peer-support service. This helpline provides information, resource referrals, and offers support to help people living with a mental health condition, their family members and caregivers, mental health providers, and the public. The staff and volunteers use their experience and training to provide guidance.

"We explain when someone is cruel or acts like a bully, you do not stoop to their level. Our motto is when they go low, you go high."

— Michelle Obama, Our First Lady

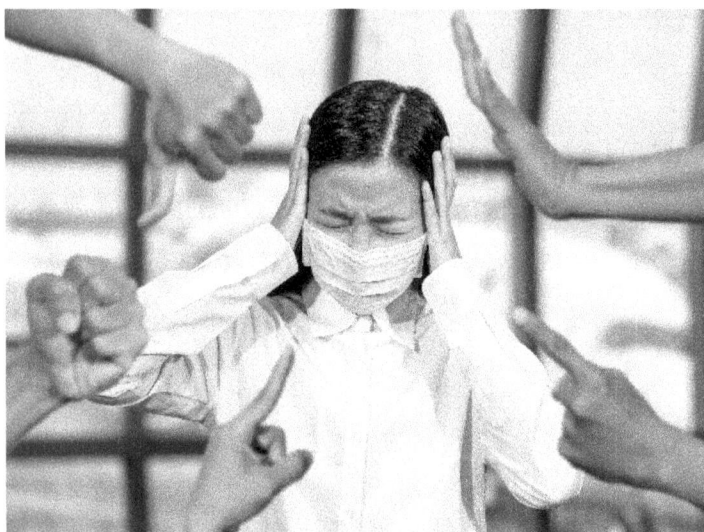

Chapter Three
Real-Life Examples

In "Obama speaks out against bullying," Nia-Malika Henderson (2011) cites President Obama regarding his experience as a victim of bullying in an excerpt from Obama's speech at the White House Bullying Prevention Convention in 2011.

As adults, we all remember what it was like to see kids picked on in the hallways or in the schoolyard. And Ihave to say, with big ears and the name that I have, I wasn't immune… I didn't emerge unscathed.But because it's something that happens a lot, and it's something that's always been around, sometimes we've turned a blind eye to the problem. We've said, 'Kids will be kids.' And so, sometimes, we overlook the real damage that bullying can do, especially when young people face harassment day after day, week after week.

In a 2012 article (Forbes.com), Leigh Steinberg speaks about the bullying crisis, calling for athletes to get involved, use their platforms, and stand up against bullying. The article highlights bullying situations. For instance, film director Lee Hirsh, who was bullied as a child, made the documentary *Bully* to expose the issue's prevalence in schools.

Steinberg recounts several situations where people were bullied so severely that they took their lives to avoid further mistreatment. Steinberg also describes a situation where a youth's attackers attempted to hang him.

John Cena became one of the biggest star professional WWE wrestlers and champions. Yet, he was bullied as a child because of his taste in music. Cena's experience makes the point that bullying knows no boundaries. He grew up in Massachusetts and was a fan of hip-hop music. As an adult, Cena became an advocate against bullying. According to a 2015 article in thesportster.com, Cena advises bullied youth to "do whatever you can to succeed." Cena's philosophy helped him overcome bullying.

Michael Phelps was constantly teased because of his long arms and big ears (ranker.com, 2019). He used what others taunted him about as the motivation for becoming a successful swimmer. Now no one bullies this winner of twenty-three Olympic gold medals.

Eva Torres, a former WWE professional wrestler, was bullied throughout high school and during her early college years (thesportster.com, 2015). Torres overcame bullying and became an instructor of self-defense classes.

These athletes used their platforms to educate and help people who have been bullied. Teaching self-defense classes or telling your story about overcoming bullying can inspire others to keep going.

How Basketball Saved My Life

It all started in middle school. I was called to read something in front of the class. The passage had the word 'strawberry' in it. I had difficulties reading and pronouncing some words, especially "str…" words. I don't even remember what the passage was about. All I remember is the word coming from my mouth sounded like SKKKRawberry, and several people were laughing. I was humiliated and embarrassed. From then on, people would insult me, calling me stupid or mocking my mispronunciations. I felt that was how they saw me—dumb and stupid. To avoid future public reading, I would ask to go to the bathroom or do something disruptive in class. I had an undiagnosed learning disability that was fodder for bullies. That was my experience.

I was dyslexic and didn't know it. The years of mistreatment and bullying from peers gradually eroded my self-esteem, further delaying my educational development. Anti-bullying intervention could have spared me the pain of those experiences.

In seventh grade, I hit a growth spurt. My godfather and a longtime family friend started coaching me on the playground basketball courts in my hometown. I joined the middle school and high school basketball and track teams. My athletic talent and abilities flourished and over-shadowed my academic difficulties, which gave me a platform to interact with others because they looked up to me (literally and figuratively). However, I was still secretly battling academic hurdles.

When I was a student-athlete at Chipola College in Marianna, Florida, an academic counselor worked with me on my reading difficulties. I learned about dyslexia, which sounded like what I had struggled with for years. Finally, I was diagnosed as dyslexic. Imagine not knowing you have a recognized and treatable learning disability.

If I had been diagnosed as a child, I could have received help in the areas where I struggled. As it happened, I did not acquire coping skills until I was diagnosed as a young adult. According to dyslexiada.org,

Dyslexia is: a specific learning disability that is neurobiological in origin. It is characterized by difficulties with accurate, fluent word recognition, poor spelling, and decoding abilities. These difficulties typically result from a deficit in the phonological component of language.

The condition presents itself in many ways. In my experience, words did not seem to flow and often appeared wavy or incomplete. In hindsight, the Hooked-on Phonics© program would have helped me greatly.

After diagnosis, I had a support system and resources to help me overcome my academic challenges related to dyslexia. As I acquired coping skills for my learning struggles and progressed in my basketball career, I was no longer a target for bullies. Instead, people wanted to be around me because of my success. Unfortunately, this is not how the story goes for many people who are bullying victims. Not everyone has a powerful support system like those who wear uniforms. Resources are often made available through athletic programs or organizations that may not be as easily accessible to other students.

The real-life stories of bullying in this chapter illustrate that neither bullies nor victims can be categorized by race, age, gender, sexual orientation, or socioeconomic status. Having a family with financial means, a 'safe' neighborhood or a quality education does not exempt a person from being bullied or becoming a bully.

People tend to look up to athletes, admire their talents and abilities, and want to hear from them. Therefore, athletes are in an ideal position to be proactive in decreasing the prevalence of bullying and preventing the development of what we now know can be lifelong problems for bullies and victims. I designed Anti-Bullying Through Sports to give athletes ideas about how to use their platform to reach those impacted by bullies.

To the world, you may be one person, but to one person, you may be the world

— Dr. Seuss

Chapter Four

R.E.A.C.H:
A Universal Solution

D r. Seuss' words capture the impact one person has on another. Such influence may be powerful enough to build a bridge, inspire a dream, or save a life. Offering a kind word or extending a helping hand can ignite hope, positivity, and inspiration in a bullied person who might not otherwise experience such positive emotions. Victims of bullying tend to have damaged self-images from bullies' efforts to ridicule, embarrass, and harass them. Kindness and words of affirmation can counter the impact of a bully's actions in meaningful ways.

REACH is an acronym for a concept embodying an anti-bullying message from the platform of athletics.

Why Athletes?

Society has long acknowledged athletes as icons of motivation, determination, overcomers, and adventurers. Athletes' iconic status grows out of numerous stories in which an individual or team triumphs in the face of adversity or learn valuable life lessons through the experience of defeat. People find such individuals and teams inspiring because the stories often reflect an enduring spirit. The celebration of sport and the athletes involved in sports comprise an important part of a healthy community.

As a case in point, let's look at a true story with a surprise ending about an athlete bullied by teammates and the broader community. Robert (Radio) Kennedy's story made it tothe big screen, *Radio* in 2003.

Radio was different from other people. He did not process information as quickly as others, nor did he speak as clearly as others.

Radio's compassion for others overshadowed his mental challenges, although teammates bullied him. To add insult to injury, students at the school. Later, community members followed the football players' lead and joined in bullying Radio.

Bullies often target anyone they perceive as "different" from their victims. Differences can take myriad forms. It may be a mental or physical disability. Other categories of difference include:

- Ethnicity
- Cultural Background
- Race
- Gender
- Age
- Sexual Orientation
- Damaged reputations caused by the spreading of compromising images or untruths

In the film, football coach Harold Jones becomes aware that the football team is bullying Radio and punishes them by making themrun laps. Much to everyone's surprise, Radio runs laps with the team, positioning himself as an ally in their punishment for mistreating him. Radio's selfless action was eye-opening for the football team. It compelled an attitude shift among those who had been unkind to him. They rethought their reasons for their antagonistic attitudes toward Radio and embraced him fully as a team member. The team's mindset and behavior shifted and had a trickledown effect throughout the school and the community. Athletes speak from a powerful platform.

What Is R.E.A.C.H?

REACH is a movement I developed to encourage and teach athletes how to use their platform against bullying. Character development through good sportsmanship and ambassadorship teaches and exemplifies the REACH acronym movement. Athletes hear these terms regularly as they prepare for competition.

R̲epresent
As an athlete, you represent your team, community, family, and friends.

Definition: Athletes may be appointed to act or speak on someone's behalf informally or in an official capacity.

E̲ncourage
Win or lose, athletes must encourage teammates to give their best.

Definition: Athletes are uniquely positioned to offer support to peers or fans, affirm others in ways that build their confidence or inspire hope in someone who has lost it.

A̲ssist
On and off the court, field, ice, or mats, athletes assist others or accept assistance. Assisting by passing a ball or puck or giving and receiving advice or guidance go hand-in-hand with being an athlete. Athletes expect to offer and receive assistance from one another, coaches, parents, and trainers.

Definition: Athletes can use their platforms to identify those needing help, offer it to them, or direct them to the needed resources.

*C*onsistent

In any sport, consistent behavior or repetition is the key to mastering fundamental skills. It is also the key to acting positively and appropriately in or out of the sports arena.

Definition: To be consistent is to remain the same. When athletes practice consistency daily on and off the court or field, they show others they are reliable. Their consistency shows others that it is safe to count on them.

*H*ope

Before, during, and after competitive events, athletes rely on hope as fuel to maintain the desire to improve continuously and, win or lose, respond in all circumstances with humility and grace.

Definition: Hope: A p e r son is hopeful when they expect something desirable to happen

Successful athletes master the principles of REACH. REACH equips them to be successful in athletics, raise awareness of the harm caused by bullying, and decrease bullying's prevalence. Athletes can use what they already have to positively impact their teams, schools, and communities. The principles of REACH allow athletes to use their platforms to influence others' lives in ways that may have long-term effects.

Imagine yourself in a situation where someone has betrayed you by revealing confidential information or sharing private images through socialmedia. Imagine how you'd feel if those who saw or heard about the posts stared, laughed, or made insulting comments to or about you. In such situations, the victim may feel overwhelmed by feelings of shame, betrayal, and embarrassment. Their self-esteem may suffer a blow. It hurts to be an object of scorn. If you can imagine yourself in such a situation, that's empathy. Sympathy means you feel sorry for someone else because something terrible happened or is happening to them. One is sympathetic when they think," I would hate it if that were happening to me. But if it were, I'd shut that bully down once and for all." One is empathetic when they think, "It's awful that Joe is being bullied. He's so shy that I imagine he doesn't know how to shut it down. I probably wouldn't know what to do if I were timid like he is." Sympathy can be compassionate or not. Empathy is always compassionate. Compassionate sympathy, empathy, and the principles of REACH position athletes to be highly effective in the anti-bullying arena.

The ability to empathize is the greatest testament to one's humanity. Indeed, the inability to empathize is one of the signs of a psychopath. Empathy facilitates connectedness with others. Empathetic people use their imaginations to understand how another person may be experiencing an event or why they are reacting in a certain way. You do not have to experience something to empathize with another person's pain, hurt, or joy. Victims of bullying sometimes receive neither empathy nor sympathy from those around them.

What Are You Willing to Do?

We must decide what we are willing to do, no matter our personality type, on our journeys for self-improvement.

REACH asks that athletes be the change they want to see.

🎥 By using the athletic platform as a billboard, you can:

- Post anti-bullying quotes and messages on your social media pages (Represent, Encourage)
- Wear attire and gear with anti-bullying messages (Represent, Encourage)
- Advocate for those who cannot advocate for themselves (Represent, Assist)
- Be kind because being nice and giving a kind word means a lot and costs nothing (Assist, Consistent)
- Educate others around you (e.g., peers, family, teammates, friends) about the effects of Bullying (Assist, Consistent)
- Volunteer (Assist, Consistent, Hope)
- Inspire others to use/explore their gifts and talents (Encourage, Hope)
- Respect differences: if everyone were the same, you would not be special (Hope)

Anti-Bullying Offense (What to Do)

📽 Use your social platforms to speak against bullying. Social media is marketing 101 in today's world. Just as you share your views on a favorite restaurant, vacation pictures, time with friends, and other things, share your anti-bullying stance. Post-anti-bullying messages in texts and on social media sites. Include photos of yourself or others at anti-bullying events. When you let others know where you stand on the issue of bullying, you create awareness of the problem. You also invite others, directly or indirectly, to help build a culture that promotes respect for everyone.

📽 Volunteer at anti-bullying events. Participating in an anti-bullying event, shows others what you are willing to represent. Athletes often attend fundraisers and events. Attending or helping to advertise an anti-bullying event brings attention to bullying.

📽 Seek help or speak out. If you need to call on others for help to address bullying, do not hesitate to do so. Principals, teachers, parents, coaches, law enforcement, and support centers can help you address bullying. Silence is not always golden. Your open disapproval of bullying can discourage bullies or potential bullies from engaging in such actions.

📽 Acknowledge and validate victims' feelings about being bullied if they share them with you. Sometimes people make subtle references to their experiences to test how someone will respond. Listen for the clues. For example, a victim might ask, "Hey, did you hear what they were calling me?" Such a question invites you to acknowledge the hurtful words or actions and find a way to address the behavior, so the victim does not suffer the effects of further bullying.

📽 Recognize bullying tactics. Bullying takes many forms, and all are harmful to the victim. Bullying tactics include:

- Belittling
- Demeaning others by name-calling
- Slurring others based on race, religion, sexual orientation, or gender identity
- Crowding around a person to intimidate them
- Publicly slandering or ridiculing
- Threatening to disclose compromising, false, or salacious information or images
- Physical violence—actual or threatened

R.E.A.C.H: A Universal Solution

Note: Sometimes, victims of bullying don't recognize that they are being bullied. They tolerate mistreatment from others because they think it means they are part of a group. They may not realize that the bullying behaviors set them apart from the group as a target for cruel treatment. There is more to belonging than being in the presence of others.

🎬 Do unto others as you would have them do unto you. The Golden Rule may seem like a tired cliché, but it matters. When we put ourselves in another person's shoes, we empathize with them. Our empathy helps us to interact with them in helpful and kind ways.

🎬 Reach out. Be kind to those around you. Acts of kindness foster healthy attitudes and relationships. Compliment someone on an accomplishment. Ask how someone's day is going. Engaging with others in simple yet genuine ways shows them they are seen, they have value, and they matter.

🎬 Be the change you want to see. Demonstrate your commitment to an anti-bullying stance. Walk your talk. What you do, say, and tolerate influences the cultures of your team, school, and community.

Anti-Bullying Defense (What not to do)

🎬 Don't encourage bullying by being a bystander or spectator.

Avoid standing around and listening to and watching a barrage of negative comments, hurtful insults, or physical attacks aimed at someone. If you are the recipient of compromising images of a person (e.g., nude photos, etc.), do not distribute the images in posts by forwarding or broadcasting in any other manner.

🎬 Don't disregard a person's expression of mistreatment as trivial or insignificant. It is often difficult for victims to share their feelings about being bullied. They tend to be ashamed of being the target of mistreatment and unsure if others will see the acts as justifiable. Such uncertainty may further damage their self-image and impair their trust in others.

🎬 Don't underestimate the potential for someone to be a bully.

🎬 Anyone can be a bully! There is no "one size fits all" description. Bullies come from all walks of life and are not bound by financial status, race, height, shape, or education level.

🎥 Don't ignore people who isolate themselves Isolation often indicates someone is unsure how to fit in. Notice who seems to be isolated and reach out. Be mindful of boundaries by asking the person if it is okay to engage with them. It may take several attempts to build trust, even when your gesture is genuine.

🎥 It is important to note that the lists of offensive and defensive moves for athletes who adopt an anti-bullying stance are not exhaustive. They offer a few suggestions for ways to intervene in bullying situations and promote anti-bullying by advocating for others who do not have a voice. Remember, anyone can be a victim; your sister, brother, friend, cousin, classmate, teammate, and so on.

Our Deepest Fear
as It Relates to REACH

The first time I heard the poem "Our Deepest Fear" by Marianne Williamson was in 2005 in the movie *Coach Carter*. The quote inspired me partly because it relates to athletics and REACH and emphasizes that bullying is not a spectator sport.

R.E.A.C.H:

Our Deepest fear is not that we are inadequate.
Our deepest fear is that we are powerful beyond measure.

Represent: It is our light, not our darkness that most frightens us. We ask ourselves, who am I to be brilliant, gorgeous, talented, fabulous? Actually, who are you not to be? You are a child of God.

Encourage: Playing small does not serve the world. There is nothing enlightened about shrinking so that other people won't feel insecure around you.

Assist: We are all meant to shine, as children do. We were born to manifest the glory of God within us. It is not just in some of us; it is in everyone.

Consistent: As we let our light shine, we unconsciously give others permission to do the same.

Hope: As we are liberated from our own fear, our presence automatically liberates others.

I encourage all athletes, coaches, parents, and community leaders to embrace REACH. Teach athletes to use the principles to promote a healthier culture and respect for others. Encourage them to get involved as anti-bullying ambassadors in their communities. Emphasize that "Anti-bullying is not a spectator sport" any more than bullying should be.

To be yourself in a world that is constantly trying to make you something else is the greatest accomplishment.

— Ralph Waldo Emerson (1803-1882)

Chapter Five

I Am Who I Am

A thletes, to understand how to use your REACH, you must first discover your distinctive personality traits and whether you identify as an introvert or an extrovert. Most athletes fall on a continuum between one or the other because of their athletic role. Derrick Rose explains his introverted nature as ""it seems like the better I play, the more attention I get, and I can't get away from it." He describes feeling forced to be both. He explains that "he hates attention, and it puts him in a weird bind." blogranker.com Article: Athletes who are definitely introverts—People in Sports Jan 27, 2020)

Let's dive in to discover what it means to be an introvert or extrovert. This will provide you with a better understanding of the two and help determine which one you relate to.

What is an introvert?

An introvert personality type refers to a person who is more comfortable focusing on their inner thoughts and ideas rather than what's happening around them.

Introverts get energized by being alone. They tend to work best independently. They can often be seen as reserved, quiet, or shy. They don't seek special attention or social engagements, as these events can leave introverts feeling exhausted and drained. Introverts are the opposite of extroverts.

– Teacherscollegesj.org/What is an introvert athlete/January 1, 2021

What is an extrovert?

Extroverts display high drive and motivation; they enjoy being the center of attention, tend to think out loud with others, and love being in large groups. Extroverts find it easy to be great speakers and are outgoing and enthusiastic. They prefer associating with people, going places, and collaborating with others.

Which are you as an athlete?
Introvert or Extrovert?

Introvert Athlete	Extrovert Athlete
Observant, thinks about specifics	Makes quick decisions
Prefers advance notice of changes	Likes surprises
Likes to get feedback in private	Likes public acknowledgment
Values close relationships, prefers spending time in solitude	Has large social network, loves being in large groups
Finds it easier to put in work in independent environments	Thrives in team-oriented & open work settings
Gains energy spending time alone	Gains energy being around other people

Do introverts like sports?

Individual sports may appeal to introverts as they require fine motor skills, precise movements, determination, and concentration. For example, introverts may become distance runners as they enjoy training alone.

- How are athletes' personalities similar and different?
- Can personality tests predict athletic performance?
- Are personality traits changeable, and would changing them even be worth the effort?

Some think bullies pick on introverts because they're quiet and reluctant to stand up for themselves. Others assume that extroverts are more likely to be bullies. But are these perceptions true?

A person's personality type is influenced by whether they are stimulated by internal stimuli, interactions with others, the environment, or situations (Healthline.com 2019). Extroverts tend to have many friends and enjoy spending time with them. Introverts enjoy spending time alone or with a friend or two and don't rely on others to validate their decisions.

Sports have become one of the most iconic cultural touchstones. Increasingly, professional athletes spread awareness about worthy causes through displays of activism on the public stages they occupy. Hence, athletes have the power to influence the minds and actions of millions of people (Tesacollective.com July 27, 2021.)

How can you use your platform as an athlete based on your personality?

Anti-Bullying Through Sports invites people to be themselves. Athletes are uniquely situated to encourage people to appreciate others' differences, making them feel safe and accepted. People are less willing to interact with others authentically and freely when they are isolated or ridiculed because of their differences. Such treatment harms a person at their core. Everyone should feel safe and proud to say, "I am who I am."

Athletes Who Top the List of Introverts

Although time alone can be difficult to find for famous professional athletes, they might need more space than their extroverted teammates. NBA champion Michael Jordan is an introvert. Tiger Woods has been criticized for being a poor team player but is an introvert. Larry Bird was shy and introverted. He wasn't one to seek the spotlight while playing for the NBA.[1]

---

[1] https://www.ranker.com/list/athletes-who-are-introverts/people-in-sports

Extrovert Athletes

- Dennis Rodman
- Ricky Hatton

📽 Athletes can approach introverts and extroverts differently to be most effective. Neither the introvert nor the extrovert should be disregarded based upon their personality characteristicsalone.

Understanding Your Platform (Uniform)

Wearing the Uniform

A uniform connects a person to a team or an organization. They represent the team ororganization by wearing the uniform. The uniform is a symbol of the environment and culture, promoting both pride and responsibility. The actions of the person wearing the uniform should reflect those values.

These are examples of people who wear uniforms, setting themselves apart as public service personnel:

Police
To Serve and Protect

Marine
The Few The Proud/Few Good Men

Firefighter
Fire and Rescue

Athletics – *past, current & future*
(We are Anti-Bullying Ambassadors)

As **athletes**, you can wear your sports uniforms to signify your REACH and roles as *anti-bullying ambassadors committed to the fight to help end bullying.*

Chapter Six

The Power of Sports & Our Responsibility

S ports can be sites of change in our communities. As we know, sports unite people from all walks of life around a common goal. They improve physical, mental, and emotional health, create opportunities for individual growth and develop confidence. People are empowered through their participation in sports.

Athletes use their uniforms in powerful ways as they stand up for what they believe is right in many situations. In the days after 9/11, all over America, people returned to work with purpose. Military, firefighters, police, and rescue teams risked their lives for no reason or reward except the admirable one to save the innocent. Here are a few situations where athletes impacted their community and beyond.

Power of Sports adopted a return to normalcy approach and it seemed at times as if it were the only thing keeping people together. It relieved those who needed it. 9/11 was still fresh in everyone's mind, but sports relieved the world from the attacks' pain, death, destruction, and debate. There were moments of silence for the victims. Players from baseball to hockey wore American flags on their jerseys. There were home runs, strikeouts, tackles, and touchdowns. There were wins and losses on an inconsequential level. There was entertainment. Sports allowed people to feel again, even if it was just for a short time.

In 2020, the world shut down due to the COVID-19 pandemic. Families were forced to isolate and remain secluded in their homes. The virtual online world was the new norm. Youth attended classes virtually, and the traditional value of family returned as we were forced to spend time together. The Power of Sports once again became a focus where, according to dosomething.org, athletes from all over the sports world donated money, led and engaged in fun activities, and used their resources (planes and social media platforms) to help care for and inform people.

The 2020 National Basketball Association (NBA) Bubble, also referred to as the Disney Bubble or the Orlando Bubble, was the isolation zone at Walt Disney World in Bay Lake, Florida, near Orlando. The NBA created the Bubble to protect its players from the COVID-19 pandemic during the final eight games of the 2019–20 season.

Before that, The Power of Sports was operative. In the ESPN docuseries "The Last Dance," the Chicago Bulls allowed a film crew to follow them as they went for their sixth NBA title in eight seasons. This resulted in a portrait of one of the sport's most celebrated teams. "The Last Dance" follows the Bulls' 1997-98 season from start to finish. The series takes its name from a phrase coined by then-Bulls Coach, Phil Jackson, who knew the season would likely be the final run for the core members of that 1990s Bulls dynasty.

Our Responsibility

REACH is an acronym. Athletes hear these terms regularly as they prepare for competition. As athletes, we are taught life lessons through sports andencouraged to compete at a high level. Dedication, desire, discipline, respect, and good citizenship are essential characteristics for athletes to successfully participate on any team. Participation in athletics is a privilege; it is not a right.

As athletes, we deal with pressure daily. We deal with social media, fans, sports networks, parents, and friends, and we are held to a higher standard. For these reasons, we need to have the memory of a goldfish to deal with criticism and constantly being in the limelight.

A goldfish?

Yes, a goldfish.

I recently learned that a goldfish forgets everything within three to ten seconds. Don't ask me how someone knows this; they just do.

Because we are held to a higher standard, we must look in the mirror and say, "I Am Who I Am," and we need to trust ourselves.

> 🎥 Our connections make athletes a perfect fit for REACH, so why not set an example and use this platform to help others?

The internet has many stories of athletes using their platforms to stand up for bullied students. The following are examples of such stories:

Athletes Help Cheerleader
with Down Syndrome Defy Bullies

https://www.npr.org/sections/thetwo-
way/2015/03/13/392782830/athletes-help-cheerleader-
with-down-syndrome-defy-bullies

Football Player Eats Lunch
with Boy with Autism After Seeing Him
Sitting Alone

https://time.com/4474258/florida-state-football-boy-
lunch-autism/

I witnessed a similar scenario with a high school student I coached. He noticed a student isolated by the other students, sitting alone, eating lunch. My player was a popular student who played basketball. The basketball player sat down with the student, had lunch with him, and they became friends.

When the isolated student's mother caught wind of what happened, she reached out to me. She shared that her son was struggling with bullying and depression and didn't want to go to school. She stated that since this the basketball player started having lunch with him, her son was beating her to the car to get to school.

> 🎬 Brothers and sisters (past, current, and future athletes), let's use our platforms to set an example of Anti-Bullying through Sports by speaking up andspeakingout.Let'sshowour communities what it truly means to put on your team's uniform and vow to stand united.

Athletic departments across the United States are implementing these concepts to ensure that every athlete is aware of the consequences of bullying.

Chapter Seven

Quick Reference to Anti-Bullying Laws and Policies

A growing number of resources are available to assist with the issue of bullying. Tools for prevention, stopping activities, counseling, and other resources are available, providing options across the United States.

📽 I recommend that athletes become familiar with their local crisis helpline and have the helpline contact information available to give the victim.

Encourage victims to call for help, assuring them they can remain anonymous. Look up your state's anti-bullying laws and add any resources you find to your toolkit for serving the anti-bullying movement.

📽️ Scan these resources so you can access your collection easily whether you're the athlete or the target of bullies.

Resources

The National Alliance on Mental Illness on NAMI.org
NAMI Helpline

The National Alliance on Mental Illness (NAMI) Helpline is a free, nationwide peer-support service. This helpline provides information, resource referrals, and offers support to help people living with a mental health condition, their family members and caregivers, mental health providers, and the public. The staff and volunteers use their experience and training to provide guidance.

What They Are Not: The NAMI Helpline is not a Hotline, Crisis Line, or Suicide Prevention Line and does not provide mental health counseling, advice, personal advocacy, or referrals to mental health providers or lawyers.

What is the difference between a helpline and a hotline? When it comes to harmful content found online, a helpline's primary focus is on children so they can support them through what they've encountered, whereas a hotline's focus is on removing the content: in this case, primarily Child Sexual Abuse Material (CSAM)

Middle school basketball players defend bullied cheerleader

CBSNEWS.com reported on March 2015 this article on the courageous behavior of these middle school basketball players. As an athlete, I hope you also feel confident as your awareness of bullying increases.

Stop Bullying on cyberbullying.org
Stop Bullying

Stopbullying.gov is anofficial website of the United States Government. The website offers a broad spectrum of information to equip advocates with information to help stopbullying. This resource suggests there are ways to stop bullying on the spot and prevent bullying by taking actions such as teaching children how to talk about bullying, creating a safe school environment, and launching a community-wide bullying prevention strategy.

Real Bullying Stories on NOPLACE4HATE.org
Real Bullying Stories

Two sisters refer to their website as no place for hate and offer what they call a safe haven. The real bullying stories are from people who experienced bullying and are willing to share the details of their struggles and victories. This resource shows visitors how a bullied person feels and invites readers' empathy.

National Suicide Prevention Lifeline at suicidepreventionlifeline.org

National Suicide Prevention Lifeline

Preventing suicide is the focus of this 24/7 resource. It is free and confidential, offering support for people who feel distressed. The prevention and crisis resources are for the individual and loved ones, and best practices are for professionals in the United States.

Bullying Laws Across America at CYBERBULLYING.org/bullying-laws
Cyberbullying Research Center

This useful resource allows you to search for cyberbullying laws in your state[2].

There are resources to help victims of bullying, their loved ones, and advocates working to stop or prevent bullying. Anyone can be a victim of bullying, including athletes. If you're an athlete (past, current, or aspiring), you can use your platform to help other bullied youth.

Become informed to advocate effectively against bullying and help bring about the change you and many others want to see. Choose a resource and use it as a starting place to educate yourself about bullying, its effects, and ways to decrease and prevent it. Familiarize yourself with as much information as possible, and join other athletes in ending the pain and harmful consequences of bullying someone.

---

[2] *Please click on any state to learn exactly what their bullying laws include.*

Conclusion

Bullying resembles a disease, but it is one we can control and cure. We can eradicate it through better education in schools and our communities.

Currently, the anti-bullying effort focuses on teachers, parents, law enforcement officers, and adults from all walks of life, including adult athletes. They are invaluable to the fight.

Anti-Bullying Through Sports is unique because it calls on youth and young athletes to use their platforms, supported by athletic departments and resources they need to be impactful. To ensure athletes do not become the targets of bullying, athletes:

- Remain connected to their athletic community.
- Receive training through the athletic departments that connect with the Anti-BullyingThrough Sports concepts.
- Use the resources provided to make wise choices when helping a bullied person feel safe and secure.

My godparents took me in when I was thirteen. They taught me many things, including the importance of representing my family and values. They also taught me about the power of sports. They inspired me to use my platform as an athlete to positively impact our community.

Athletes who embrace Anti-Bullying Through Sports recognize the principles of the program from their involvement in sports and how they transfer to the anti-bullying effort. When playing offense, reading the defense is a powerful strategy in sports and in the fight against bullying.

Athletes' voices can be heard and therefore used to change the lives of those being bullied. Vow to stand united in character and declare your responsibility to use your platform positively to help others.

This book is a call for action directed to past, current, and future athletes and coaches to continue building momentum to end bullying. The strategies discussed throughout this book can equip people to help make schools and communities safe havens for our youth.

Anti-Bullying Through Sports, the book, is one of those tools. While the book focuses explicitly on athletes' platforms, anyone can adapt the information. Those working in management at a Fortune 500 company are a team. They could use the concepts in this book to campaign against bullying in the workplace or elsewhere.

Often what people are going through is unknown. This book can help show athletes how to use their platform to help others. On the field, offensive players read the defense and use the information to make headway toward victory. An athletic coach can adjust the next play based on his reading of what happens on the field. When the ball is in the air, both offense and defense stand a 50/50 chance of grabbing the ball while it is in the air.

The same is true when identifying bullying situations and adjusting strategies for intervention. Read the situation, and decide how to proceed based on the information presented in this resource.

The person intervening is safe because they can choose when or if to implement the strategies. A person may observe a situation and take no action. Later, however, they could post a message on Facebook or Twitter that says, "I wish people would be more respectful." Indirect statements are also a way to REACH someone to build a bridge, inspire hope or a dream, and perhaps even save a life.

CERTIFICATE
OF COMPLETION

PROUDLY PRESENTED TO

Anti-Bullying Ambassador

4J's Sports, Inc.

Anti-Bullying through Sports, LLC

We're calling all past, current, and future athletes to continue building on this momentum to help end bullying.

The Pledge

We want to change the lives of those being bullied.

We vow to STAND UNITED in character and our responsibility be known.

Our hope is that our voice will be heard:

We are Anti-Bullying Ambassadors

How Did You Get Started with REACH?

– Interviewed by: Yvette Ward

My wife put my son in an AAU Program. I watched the practices and the kids leaving the practices. They talked loudly, used profanity, and did not hold the door open for their elders. After hearing me express my concern several times about their behavior, my wife encouraged me to start an AAU Program. I decided it would not be solely about basketball. In addition, the athletes learned about bullying through the program I later called REACH. They learned about etiquette, including taking their moms on dates to learn how to treat women. The movement aimed to teach young athletes the importance of character development through good sportsmanship and ambassadorship in representing their team to the community through service programs and competitions. I taught them to exemplify the principles in each pillar of REACH as necessary to successfully participate.

Our motto:
I am who I am, time to REACH

My anti-bullying movement, REACH, helped boys reach out and use their platform to help others. Over the years, I developed the concept. Today, REACH is different than it was back then. This book is a tool focused on Anti-Bullying Through Sports.

What is your expectation of REACH?

My expectation is for all coaches, and athletes to use their platform to make a difference off the court/field. For example, in the game of basketball if I pass the ball that's an assist, we can apply this in the same way by opening the door for someone we may not know. I want to try to change the perspective and mindset of athletes, and encourage the fans and community to support them through anti-bullying through sports.

Who is the most influential person in your life?

My grandmothers (Lola), big mama (Marjorie) and granny (Susan) because of the values they instilled in me from work ethic, giving back, family values and helping others.

What was school like growing up, and were you a victim bullying? How did you rise above?

Well, first, it was difficult not knowing what I was dealing with, not having the resources, and being raised by a grandmother who didn't have much schooling. She did what she could, but I often wondered if it was that way with everyone else's household. I thought it was.

I didn't understand because I would study, read, and think I knew the information. But I often failed tests, and verbal spelling tests in front of the class were even worse. I was teased and made fun of early on, but it didn't feel so bad because of my personality, character, and how I treated people.

What woke me up was a fifth-grade teacher who told me I would never amount to anything. I still carry thatto this day because one of her statements was that a black kid with no parents would be either in jail or selling drugs. I held on to that and used it as one of my motivations.

When I was introduced to basketball, everything changed. I wouldn't say I was a bully; I was more of a protector because I saw some of the abuse my aunt and sisters went through when they were dating, and I was protective of people.

I always say basketball is what I did but not who I am. That's only partially true because basketball helped make me who I am. I may not have met my wife, I wouldn't have met my best friend, and I may never have been diagnosed. Basketball took me out of Choctaw County and gave me access to the resources to diagnose me, help me learn ways to deal with dyslexia, and learn about myself. There, I overcame being ashamed. Early on in my life, it was a struggle, but when I was introduced to basketball, it changed my life inmany ways.

As a basketball player, did you experience bullying?

No, not from the moment I reached high school. Think about it this way I'm 6'6"and played with teammates just as tall or taller walking beside me. The way athletes are viewed, no one bothers them and if they were, the rest of the team would come to their defense. This kind of loyalty influenced the model for Anti-Bullying through Sports.

Tell me anything you want your audience to hear and know about you and what you're doing?

I'm not perfect; my life was hard. I didn't quit, and I didn't give up. To see where I came from and what I had to overcome, some people would say, "Wow, you're still here." Listen, I'm still trying to make a difference and impact, mainly because of the words I heard from my grandmother and my godparents at a younger age: *"Treat people like you want to be treated and speak up for those who can't."* So that keeps me going.

I'm eager to please, and I'm serious about appreciation. I had families from my hometown who supported me. So, I feel it would be hypocritical to turn back when they invested time and money to support me and didn't ask for anything in return. This recognition is one of my ways of giving back to them. You see my name now, but when I look at it, I see all of them.

I have a different mindset, and because of my learning disorder, I see many things differently than most people. I thought it was normal, but now I look at it and realize it's a gift. My main goal is to move forward and help people. If I can prevent one person's death by suicide due to bullying, then I've done my job.

IF YOU APPRECIATE SOMEONE
give them their flowers while
THEY CAN STILL SMELL THEM

Acknowledgments

Heavenly Father, thank you for loving me, showing me my worthiness, and pursuing me. Thank you for giving me a vision filled with purpose, guiding me on this journey, and humbling me. Without you, there would be no me.

* * *

Thank you to my wife, Kisha, for your endless support on this journey. I am forever grateful to you for reading early drafts, offering advice on content, and always standing by my side. Thank you, my love, for being a pillar in my life and my solid foundation.

* * *

A very special thank you to my children Juon, Jannee' Josiah, Jazmin, and my grandkids, Jayla, Isaiah, Jordan, Christopher, Jalen, Jaahren, and my future grandkids. I truly believe you are in my life to help me on my journey. You are there for me when I need comfort, kindness, motivation, and purpose. You are the real inspiration for this book. Words cannot express how blessed I am. I love you.

* * *

My beautiful grandmother, Ms. Lola Ruffin, you are the foundation of my being. You raised me like your son, taking me in when I was six weeks old. We didn't have much, butI was rich in things that money cannot buy— solid values and the life lessons you taught me. I miss you.

I wish you were here to share these moments with me. May you rest knowing that I continuously strive to make you and those I love proud.

* * *

I never imagined writing a book would be so challenging and rewarding at the same time. This would not have been possible without my godparents, Neil & Clemmie Manior. You took me under your wing, loved me, and gave me the confidence and support I lacked as a young child. You showed me the true meaning of unconditional love, and I am eternally grateful for both of you.

* * *

To my older sisters Rena and Barbara, there's never a single day that I wish you weren't my sisters. We had a rough start in life with the passing of our mom. I was only 2 years old and don't know anything about her but what you two shared with me. You are the most beautiful, caring, loving persons I know, and I love being your younger brother. I'm so lucky to have sisters like you, and I thank God for blessing me with such wonderful sisters like you. Thanks for being there for me, from my greatest moment to my darkest moments; thank you for just being you. My godsisters, Brittney Marzetta, Judie Bee, and godbrother, Cedrick Manior, thank you for accepting me as your big brother and sharing your parents' love, guidance, and values with me. I am proud to be a part of the Manior family.

* * *

My best friend, Al Pinkens, bro, you were by my side through my successes and, even more so, my struggles. Who would have thought our paths crossing in college over thirty years ago would grow into a relationship that exemplifies true friendship? Our competitive natures and trash-talking challenges drove us to where we are today. (Don't forget that you still cannot beat me, bro.)

* * *

Ricky Dukes, my passion for sports and paying it forward started with you. When I was ten, I planted myself on a curb one Saturday morning and told the older kids playing basketball, "I got next." You chose me when no other kids picked me to play on their team. You changed my life that day. You fueled my passion for basketball and modeled behavior that showed me how one person's actions can affect another's life.

* * *

Coach Kermit Davis, you saw a young 6'6" man passionate about basketball. You saw an athlete hungry to learn, grow, and succeed at the sport. You pushed me to my limits, encouraged me, and made me see the infinite possibilities that the world offered me on and off the court. Thank you for mentoring me and seeing my potential.

* * *

FC Kimbrough, you are like a big brother to me. During my youth, you kept me humble and down to earth. You have been the voice of reason in my life for many years.

Thank you for always being present when I have needed a listening ear, words of encouragement, or guidance.

* * *

My in-laws, Willie Carl and Teresa Merrell, thank you for your unconditional support of my vision. I am grateful for your love and guidance on this journey.

* * *

Mike Damelio, my Italian brother, you have been with me in some of my darkest moments, constantly pushing and encouraging me because you knew brighter days were ahead. You invested in me when I was told I would never play basketball again because of what was thought to be a career-ending injury. The time and effort you dedicated to rehabbing me physically also helped me mentally during that dark time. You single-handedly brought me back stronger than ever. Thank you for being the light along the way.

* * *

Seaford Marzette, Jr., you set the tone for me to be a great player in my high school days, sacrificing your time in the spotlight to share it with me. Thank you for seeing in me what I didn't see in myself. I remember the high school game against our rival school rival in my junior year. You went against the coach's play, risking getting benched, so I could shine. Your decision that day taught me what it means to be part of a team. The kindness behind it showed me what it means to be a true friend.

* * *

To Onnie "Aunt Honey" Dukes Williams, Florine "Rine" Dukes Anthony, and Ann Spears, thanks for accepting me into the Dukes/Williams family and showing me love. Iremember when you told me, "You are a part of this family and we love you. Let me know if anyone treats you otherwise." Your words of inclusion were powerful to me. I love you all. Thank you for seeing me, accepting me, and loving me.

* * *

To the victims of bullying and their families, if I could stand up for each of you and protect you from bullying and the harm it causes, I would. My mission is to do everything I can to educate people about the harmful effects of bullying in innocent people's lives and, one day, stop it. You are loved. I am here. I see you.

Special Thanks to:

- The Dukes/Williams Family
- Sheria Barron
- Coach Scott Taylor
- Coach Murry Bartow
- James Barnes (L.B.)
- Susan Small (Granny)
- George & Sandra Simmons & Family
- The Hildreth/Ruffin (family)
- Rickey Hampton
- Willie & Helen Mc Rand
- Tony Arroyo
- John Arroyo
- Chris Ward
- Ted Fowler
- Terry &Lisa Bryant
- Thomas Roscoe, Jr.
- Shaquille O'Neal
- Vincent L. Carter
- Yvette Ward
- Billy Jefcoat
- Team Ted
- Loretta Ingraham (staff)
- Samuel (Cisco) Berry
- CCHS Class of 1991
- Coach Arthur Vincent
- Coach Miguel Martinez
- Chipola Jr. College Teammates
- Troy University Teammates
- Charles Barkley
- CCHS Teammates
- Vigo Spain Teammates
- Riverview Hurricane Family
- Coach David Felix
- Coach Don Maestra
- Phi Beta Sigma Fraternity
- Darrell Armstrong
- Zeta Phi Beta Sorority
- Mike Trigg
- Coach Milton H. Johnson

- Calvary Chapel of Brandon
- Uncle Herbert Small
- Mr. Vernon Underwood
- Coach Charlie Thompson (track coach)
- Roosevelt and Marjorie "Big Mommy" Barron
- Clinton Smith & Family
- Dr. Rick Davila
- David and Heather Howes
- Shon Ewens
- Damon and Laura Dye
- Chris and Cindy Sorfarelli
- Tony and Teresia Cherry
- Ricky Gallon
- Kara Pinkins
- Win and Ronda Case
- MTSU Family/Players
- Paul and Renee Gregory
- Jamey and Gayle Westbrook
- Jeff James
- Coach Mike and Kelly Alice
- Coach Rodney King
- City of Tampa
- Robert and Kay Trammell
- Riverview Boys and Girls Club Board
- Amanda Rich
- Grace Christian School of Valrico FL.
- Coach Terrence Robinson
- Vigo Spain Community

Writing a book about something you are passionate about is a surreal and humbling process. Many people inspired me to write this book. I apologize if I have left anyone off this list. Much love to everyone who played a role in my life and this project. Releasing this book is just the beginning.

References

Marianna Williamson "(A Return to Love)
March 15, 1996

StopBullying.gov

Blog.securly.com

Endcyberbullying.org

Forbes.com/feb.21,2013 article on Alice G.
Walton (published in JAMA Psychiatry)

Washington Post March 11,2011 By:
Nia Malika Henderson Title: Obama speaks out
against bullying says, I wasn't immune

Dyslexiada.org

The Sportster.com/John Cena 2015 article

Ranker.com/ June 14,2019 Michael Phelps (6
athletes who were bullied

Ranker.com/ Jan.27,2020 Athletes Who are
Definitely Introverts

Eve Torres The sportster.com/2015 article self
defense

Dr. Seuss/ to the world you may be one-person
Quotable Quote

The 2003 Movie Radio

About the Author

Fred Spencer is a former professional basketball player who played in Vigo, Spain. He is a graduate of Springfield College and played college basketball at Chipola Jr. College in Marianna, Florida and Troy University in Troy, Alabama. He is a business professional and educator.

Some essential details about Fred:

- He grew up in the small town of Pennington, Alabama, which he affectionately calls "the country."
- He was teased from elementary to late middle school because of his poor reading and writing abilities.
- He grew in stature to become 6'6".

He became a prominent basketball team member and was liberated from insults andcriticism simply because he was a student-athlete. As a college athlete, he was diagnosed with dyslexia and felt he received the necessary assistance because he was a student-athlete, which helped him overcome the condition. Basketball helped him accept his limitations.

He is a leader and influencer in his community and for his student-athletes.

Fred developed the Anti-Bullying Through Sports concept and is pleased to present it to you.

Anti-Bullying
"Did You Know" Puzzle

ACROSS

5 As a result of bullying, A third of victims go on to develop social anxiety and _____.

6 _____is the color for anti-bullying awareness.

8 The H in REACH stands for?

12 ____.are frequently thought of as being bullies and mean.

13 Which type of bullying is missing from the list: physical, verbal, social, sexting and _____.

14 Short name for Center for Disease control.

DOWN

1 What non-profit organization developed the anti-bullying through sports program?

2 People often mistake bullying for being_____.

3 Speak up and ____. ____. against bullying.

4 Depression and ____. ____. are on the rise among the youth.

7 _____is anti-bullying month.

8 If you or someone you care about is feeling overwhelmed with sadness, anxiety, depression, or self-harm you can call your local _____.

9 Bullying isn't a _____ sport.

10 As an athlete, you have the _____ to impact the lives of others.

11 _____ is one of the top causes of death for teenagers in the US – according to the CDC.

Anti-Bullying "Did You Know" Puzzle

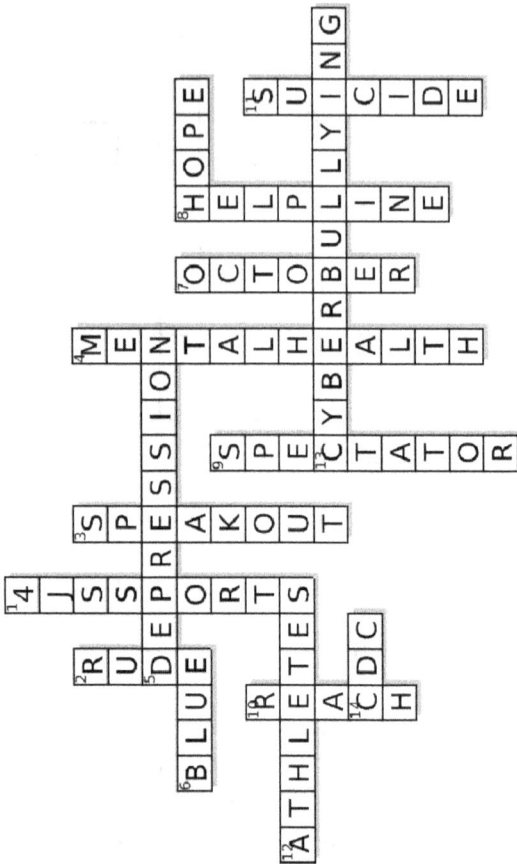

WORD BANK: 4JSSPORTS, ATHLETES, BLUE, CDC, CYBERBULLYING, DEPRESSION, HELPLINE, HOPE, MENTALHEALTH, OCTOBER, REACH, RUDE, SPEAKOUT, SPECTATOR, SUICIDE

Contact Fred Spencer

Fred Spencer is also an
Internationally Acclaimed Athlete and Speaker.

Topics he speaks on include:
- Anti-Bullying
- Athletic Coaching
- Mindset
- Motivational

Booking enquiries or
Order bulk or additional copies of this book, contact:
4JsSports@gmail.com

Follow Fred on social media:
Instagram: 4JsSports | Facebook: 4JsSports
#4JsSports | #AntiBullyingThroughSports
www.4JsSports.com

All books available on:
www.4JsSports.com
Amazon.com | Barnes & Noble

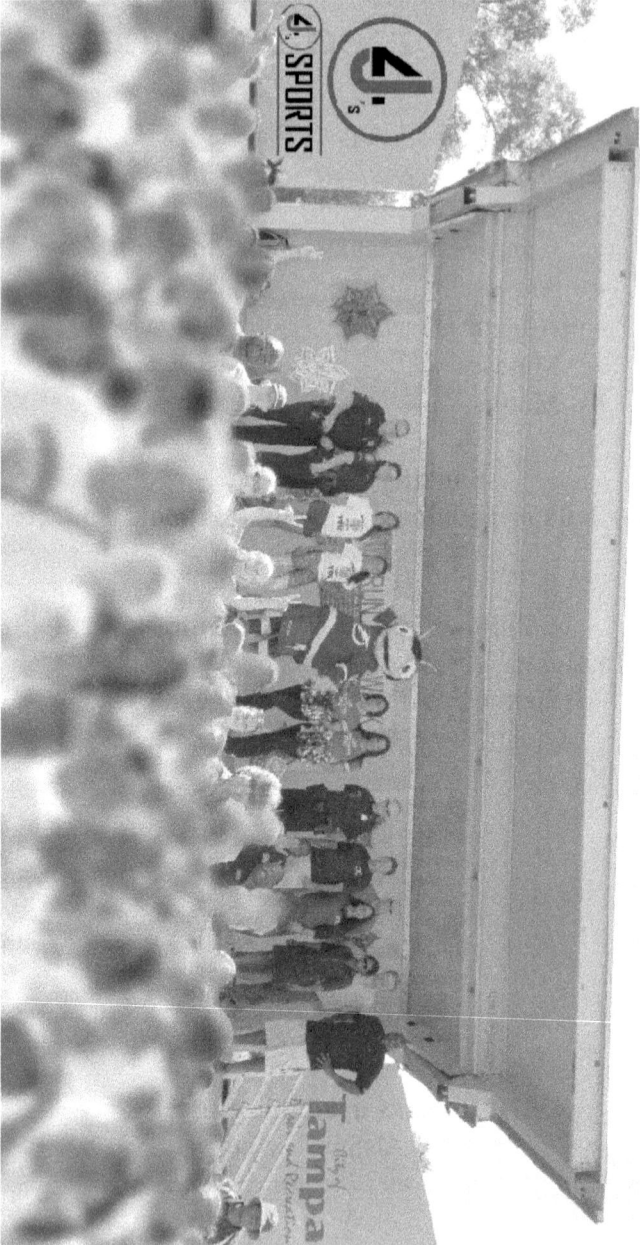

www.ingramcontent.com/pod-product-compliance
Lightning Source LLC
Chambersburg PA
CBHW072237290326
41934CB00008BB/1327